THIS JOURNAL BELONGS TO:

____